I0845823

Non-deterministic Finite Automata

Translating Theory to Code

Table of Contents

Chapter 1. Introduction

In this engaging Special Report, we delve into the fascinating and complex world of Non-deterministic Finite Automata (NFA), a fundamental concept in the realm of Computer Science Theory. Rather than leaving you stuck in abstract thought, we bridge the gap between theory and practicality by providing methods to translate these theoretical constructs into functional lines of code. Written with an approachable style, we bring light to this sometimes intimidating field, stripping away the mystique and making it an accessible and rewarding endeavor for anyone who wishes to gain a deeper understanding of this core computational concept. Whether you are a seasoned developer, an aspiring computer scientist, or someone simply intrigued by the intricacies of how computers process information, this report stands as a valuable insight into the heart of computational theory. It's time to unearth the beauty of Non-deterministic Finite Automata: Translating Theory to Code.

Chapter 2. Understanding the Basics of Non-deterministic Finite Automata

Non-deterministic Finite Automata (NFA) takes its role as one of the core concepts in the realm of theoretical computer science. Its beauty lies in the range of possibilities it offers, traversing paths in any possible direction as opposed to following a single defined route.

NFAs form the building blocks of algorithms. Therefore, a strong grasp of the fundamental understanding of the functionality of non-deterministic finite automata lies at the heart of mastering the art of computer science.

2.1. Beginnings of Non-deterministic Finite Automata

NFA, as an abstract machine, can be in one or several states at any given instant. Unlike deterministic finite automata (DFA), NFA can transition from one state to another through multiple paths. Each state transition is governed by a transition function that takes an input symbol and the current state to arrive at a possible set of next states—this is the crux that sets it apart from deterministic finite automata.

Consider a system as simple as tossing a coin. When modeled deterministically (akin to a DFA), a coin toss results in two possibilities—heads or tails. However, in an NFA representation, at any given point, you're considering both possibilities simultaneously.

2.2. The Mathematical Model

NFAs are represented as a 5-tuple $(Q, \Sigma, \delta, q0, F)$, where:

- Q is a finite set of states.

- Σ is a finite set of input symbols (the alphabet).

- δ is the transition function ($\delta: Q \times \Sigma \to P(Q)$).

- $q0$ is the starting state.

- F is a set of accepting or final states.

The transition function, δ, operates on a state and an input symbol, and yields a set of states. This is a key departure from DFAs, where δ would define a single next state.

2.3. Exploring State Transitions

State transitions are core to understanding NFAs. The presence of ε-transitions (transitions that occur without consuming an input symbol) and multiple possible next states are two striking peculiarities that make NFAs powerful and appealing.

The transition function is able to handle ε-transitions. If q is a state in Q and X is a subset of Q, then if q☐X, we get an ε-move, and if q☐δ(Z, ε) for some state Z in X, we get an ε-transition. ε-transitions offer flexibility. They aid in converting between regular expressions and finite automata, a property employed while using regular expression search in text editors.

2.4. The Language of NFAs

NFAs recognize the class of languages known as regular languages. A language recognized by an NFA is defined as the set of strings that, when processed by the NFA, land it in an accepting state starting from the initial state.

Each string symbol can potentially alter the current state of the NFA. The final state (or lack thereof) that the automaton ends up in after processing all input symbols determines whether the sequence of symbols makes up a valid string in the recognized language. If the final landing state upon processing the string is within set F of final states, the string is considered valid.

2.5. Building an NFA

As with any theoretical construct, the best way to gain a deep understanding of NFAs is to try your hand at designing them. Let's demonstrate this through the example of designing an NFA that accepts any binary string ending in "101".

Your NFA must have four states—q0 (start state), q1, q2, and q3 (the final state)—and should accept input from $\Sigma = \{0, 1\}$. The transitions should be defined as follows:

- $\delta(q0, 1) = \{q0, q1\}$
- $\delta(q0, 0) = \{q0\}$
- $\delta(q1, 0) = \{q2\}$
- $\delta(q1, 1) = \{\}$
- $\delta(q2, 1) = \{q3\}$
- $\delta(q2, 0) = \{\}$
- $\delta(q3, 1) - \{q1\}$
- $\delta(q3, 0) = \{\}$

Note how the NFA is allowed to be in either of multiple states at a single point in time. Also note how some transitions do not have a signaling instance. These instances represent the primary differences between DFAs and NFAs and highlight some of the central design considerations necessary when designing an NFA.

To construct NFAs, one must grasp the art of considering simultaneous possibilities—an elusive skill that allows our theoretical machine to move from the world of the simple deterministic coin toss to navigating complex graphs of possibilities.

2.6. The Journey Ahead

Handling NFAs requires fluency in tackling the scope of outcomes rather than one clear trajectory. This journey through the basic understanding of NFAs provides a launchpad to delve deeper into this rich field. In the upcoming discussions, we will rigorously explore the ways to convert these theoretical constructs into lines of functioning codes, thereby bridging the gap between theory and application. Through this lens, we step into the intriguing world of computational theory, where concepts are not as elusive as they seem. Instead, they become engaging puzzles to solve, better equipping us to explore the beauty and intricacies of the machines we use in everyday life.

In essence, understanding non-deterministic finite automata serves as a foundation to demystify the much-exalted theoretical computer science, rendering it an engaging and approachable field.

Chapter 3. Diving Deeper into NFA: State and Transition

Consider a complex collection of pathways, each leading to various destinations based on the decisions made at the junctions. This can be seen as a fundamental representation of what a Non-deterministic Finite Automaton (NFA) does. A theoretical abstraction in computer science, an NFA is a mathematical model of computation. It is a finite state machine where, for each pair of state and input symbol, there can be several possible next states. All operations are deterministic in essence and are defined in terms of sets of states.

3.1. Unveiling the State in NFA

In the context of NFAs, a state constitutes the condition of a system at any point. Each state depicts a specific configuration at which a system can exist. An NFA, by the nature of its function, has to have a finite number of states.

In every NFA, there is a start state (or initial state) from where any input is processed. There also can be one or more final states or accept states that depict a successful run of the system on the given input.

Coding this in a programming language might simply involve using an enumerated datatype to represent individual states or even using integers if the states don't have any semantic meaning.

For example, an NFA with states q0 (start state), q1, q2 (accept state) might be represented in Python as:

```python
class State:
    INITIAL = 'q0'
```

```python
    INTERMEDIATE = 'q1'
    FINAL = 'q2'
```

But in a real-world scenario, the complexity of the states and transitions could be much higher and it would need a more efficient data structure to map the states and transitions. This is where data structures like hash maps come in handy, which brings us to the next section.

3.2. Transitioning in NFA

A transition in an NFA is a shift from one state to another, in response to an input symbol. Every state in an NFA is associated with multiple transitions that are determined by the input symbols. Unlike in deterministic finite automata (DFAs), in an NFA for each pair of a state and an input symbol, the system can transition to any number of states or no state at all.

Transitions in NFAs can be represented using a transition function, which is a mapping from the cross product of the set of all states and the set of all input symbols to the power set of states.

To encode this transition function in a programming language, data structures like dictionaries (a.k.a., hash maps) can be used due to their fast look-up time complexity.

Here's an example in Python:

```python
transition_function = {
    (State.INITIAL, '0'): [State.INITIAL,
State.INTERMEDIATE],
    (State.INITIAL, '1'): [State.INITIAL],
    (State.INTERMEDIATE, '0'): [State.FINAL],
    (State.INTERMEDIATE, '1'): [],
    (State.FINAL, '0'): [State.FINAL],
```

```
        (State.FINAL, '1'): [State.FINAL]
}
```

In this dictionary, each key is a pair of a state and an input symbol, and the corresponding value is a list of next states.

3.3. Implementing NFA as a Class

Bringing the two important constructs together, an example of implementing NFA as an object-oriented class would look like:

```
class NFA:
    class State:
        INITIAL = 'q0'
        INTERMEDIATE = 'q1'
        FINAL = 'q2'

    transition_function = {
        (State.INITIAL, '0'): [State.INITIAL,
State.INTERMEDIATE],
        (State.INITIAL, '1'): [State.INITIAL],
        (State.INTERMEDIATE, '0'): [State.FINAL],
        (State.INTERMEDIATE, '1'): [],
        (State.FINAL, '0'): [State.FINAL],
        (State.FINAL, '1'): [State.FINAL]
    }

    def __init__(self):
        self.current_states = {State.INITIAL}

    def transition(self, symbol):
        next_states = set()
        for state in self.current_states:
```

```python
        next_states.update(self.transition_function.get((state,
symbol), []))
        self.current_states = next_states

    def run(self, input_string):
        for symbol in input_string:
            self.transition(symbol)
        return State.FINAL in self.current_states
```

With the NFA class, you can model an NFA and simulate its operation
with an input string. The transition method updates the current
states according to the input symbol and the transition function, and
the run method determines if the NFA accepts the given input string.

Despite the seeming complexity of the subject, NFAs are truly
beautiful in their ability to model complex computations, making
them a vital concept to understand in computer science. Translating
them to code not only gives us a practical understanding, but also
equips us with tools to solve real-world problems that are best
modeled by non-deterministic computations.

Chapter 4. The Alphabet of NFA: Symbols and Directions

To comprehend the behavior of Non-deterministic Finite Automata (NFA), it is essential to understand its fundamental alphabet - the symbols and directions it uses. This chapter offers an elaborate discussion on these critical components of NFA.

The first stop on our journey is understanding what constitutes symbols in NFAs context, thus, making up its alphabet. Then, we'll explore the directions they signify, which form the structure and shape of the path traversed by the DFA.

4.1. Elements of the NFA Alphabet: The Symbols

An Alphabet, in theoretical computational context, refers to a finite set of symbols. These symbols act as the most basic building blocks of all the computations that are carried out by an automaton.

In Non-deterministic Finite Automata, an alphabet (commonly denoted by the Greek letter Σ or sigma) is a finite, non-empty set of symbols. These symbols serve as inputs fed into the DFA during its operation. For example, for a simple NFA designed to recognize binary strings, the alphabet {0, 1} would suffice. Here, each symbol - '0' or '1', serves to trigger a transition from one state to another within the NFA.

4.2. Understanding Symbol Usage

A symbol's purpose in an NFA is not merely to represent a physical piece of data. Instead, each symbol holds a dual functionality: it can both influence the state of the machine and denote specific transitions.

The state of the machine can be understood as the position or condition of the NFA at any given point in the computation process. Simply put, it is where the NFA "is", metaphorically speaking, in its journey through the input string. And it is by following the transitions dictated by each input symbol that the NFA traverses this journey.

Every symbol in the NFA's alphabet can cause the machine to change its state. This transition may be to one or more possible states or might even result in looping back to the current state. The actual operation, heavily depends on the NFA's rule set.

4.3. Directions in an NFA

Understanding directions in a Non-deterministic Finite Automaton is no less important than comprehending its symbols. In fact, the duo forms an integrated system and is inseparable in the world of NFAs.

These directions are essentially the paths that an automaton takes from one state to another, triggered by the input symbols it reads. For instance, if your NFA consists of states {A, B, C} and symbol set {0, 1}, there may be a rule saying that being in state 'A' and reading symbol '0' leads the automaton to transition to state 'B'.

4.4. Flexibility of Directions

One of the defining characteristics of an NFA is the ability of each state to have multiple ways of responding to a particular symbol. This non-deterministic property allows for several possible transitions for the same input symbol. In practical terms, this means that, given a specific state and input symbol, an NFA might transition to any one of several potential states, including possibly the state it is currently in.

Consider a scenario where our NFA is in state 'A', and we read the symbol '0'. If the rules of the NFA specify that state 'A' can transition to either state 'B' or state 'C' when reading a '0', the automaton may choose either path. This adds a remarkable depth of possibility and flexibility in the operations of an NFA.

4.5. Implications of ε-transitions

A unique aspect of NFAs is the allowance of ε-transitions (epsilon transitions), a luxury not provided in DFAs. An ε-transition allows the automaton to move from one state to another without consuming any input symbols. This characteristic further adds to the flexibility of NFAs, allowing them to essentially "skip" states without needing any particular symbol.

To put into perspective, consider again the NFA with states {A, B, C}. If there is an ε-transition between 'A' and 'B', our NFA could move from 'A' to 'B' without reading any symbol from the input string. However, it's important to note that not all NFAs necessarily contain ε-transitions, and their inclusion depends heavily on the nature of the problem the NFA is designed to solve.

4.6. Conclusion

By appreciating the role of symbols and directions in NFAs context, understanding these computational constructs becomes substantially less daunting and more intriguing. Symbols, as the basic elements of an NFA's input, hold a dual functionality of influencing the state or condition of the NFA and denoting specific transitions. This symbiotic play of symbols and directions acquired through them, give the NFA its mystifying non-determinism, lending to it an edge of unpredictability and versatility, making it a robust and essential asset in the realm of computational theory. We can now forge ahead, armed with a firmer understanding of these critical components, to further tackle the mysteries this abstract machine holds.

Chapter 5. Establishing Difference between Deterministic and Non-deterministic Finite Automata

Before discussing the inner workings and details of Non-deterministic Finite Automata (NFA), we need to take a step back and venture into the territory of its deterministic counterpart - Deterministic Finite Automata (DFA). Although the two may seem overwhelmingly complex at first glance, once we break down their essential components and dive into their distinct attributes, you'll grasp their differences and better understand how they function.

5.1. Understanding Deterministic Finite Automata

The word 'deterministic' implies that the outcome is predetermined or certain. This notion aligns perfectly with Deterministic Finite Automata (DFA), a theoretical model of computation used extensively in computer science. Like a well-choreographed dance, DFAs follow certain strict criteria for operation:

1. Each DFA begins at a predetermined start state.

2. It moves from one state to another upon reading input characters.

3. There is only one transition for each symbol at every state.

Let's consider an example. Imagine you have a DFA that determines whether a binary number input is divisible by 2. Your DFA would start at the initial state (let's call it state A). Here, we determine that every state transition driven by the input '0' to this state (since adding a 0 to the end of a binary number effectively multiplies it by 2). In contrast, if the input is '1', the DFA transitions to another state (state B), indicating the binary number is not divisible by 2. In this way, there's only one possible next state for each character input at each state.

5.2. Transitioning to Non-deterministic Finite Automata

Now with knowledge of DFAs, let's muddy the waters a bit and introduce some uncertainty. NFAs, unlike their deterministic counterparts, do not adhere to strict state transition rules. In the realm of NFAs:

1. They also start at a predetermined initial state.

2. They can transition to zero, one, or multiple next states for each input character.

3. They can even transition without any input (known as ε or epsilon-transitions).

Let's re-imagine our binary divisibility problem in the context of NFA. You might construct an NFA where, upon encountering an input of '1', it could remain in state A (staying divisible by 2 if the next digit is 0) or move to state B (if the next digit is 1). So, if your input string was '1010', the NFA could move from state A to state B with the first '1', stay in state B with the next '0', and so on. The idea is that the NFA simultaneously explores all possible state transitions and considers an input string as accepted if any of those possible paths end in an acceptable state. This non-determinism opens up exciting and complex pathways within your computation models.

5.3. Comparing DFAs and NFAs

In a nutshell, DFAs maintain a single state at any given point, while NFAs manage a set of states. But let's dig deeper into the significant differences.

1. *State transitions*: As stated earlier, DFAs transition to exactly one state for each input from any given current state, while NFAs have the flexibility to transition into any number of states, including zero, for a particular input.

2. *Epsilon transitions*: NFAs have an added feature that further distinguishes them from DFAs - epsilon transitions. These are transitions that don't require any input (thus designated by ε) and allow you to progress from one state to another.

3. *Computation and resource usage*: Generally, DFAs are faster to compute given their deterministic nature but are relatively restrictive. On the other hand, NFAs may spend more resources exploring multiple paths, but they offer more flexibility and are advantageous in certain computational scenarios, such as regular expression matching and compiler design.

4. *Ease of Design*: When it comes to design, NFAs tend to be simpler and more intuitive to formulate than DFAs, particularly for complex languages. However, this does not mean that NFAs are superior or inferior to DFAs. It's all about using the right tool for the right task!

5. *Equivalence*: The most fascinating factor is that for every NFA, an equivalent DFA can be constructed. The opposite also holds. Hence, both NFAs and DFAs are equivalent power-wise. However, the process converting an NFA into a DFA, called determinization, can lead to an exponential growth in states, potentially complicating the system.

There you have it; these distinguishing traits illustrate the diverse behaviors of DFAs and NFAs, making each invaluable in various aspects of computing. However, their shared DNA provides the foundation for their capabilities, allowing them to capture the magic of computational thinking. We hope this explanation helps in your journey to unearth the beauty and power inherent in the vast world of automata. In subsequent sections, we will delve deeper into the practical side of these concepts and see how theory translates seamlessly into code.

Chapter 6. The Power of ε-transitions in NFA

The ε-transition, also known as the epsilon or empty transition, holds an intriguing status within the context of Non-deterministic Finite Automata (NFA). On the surface, it may appear puzzling – a transition that requires no input from an alphabet of symbols – yet it is a pillar that allows for greater possibilities and flexibility within NFA design.

6.1. Introducing ε-transitions

Familiarizing ourselves with the concept of ε-transitions, we first need to grasp that it represents a unique sort of transition - one that allows the finite automaton to alter states without consuming any symbol or input sequence.

A ε-transition can be graphically symbolized as an arrow from one state to another, labeled with the Greek letter ε or sometimes λ or even Ø, indicating no input symbol is read during this transition. In terms of functional context, such a transition signifies that a NFA can shift from the present state to the next without needing any input.

6.2. Understanding The Role of ε-transitions

Now that we've established what a ε-transition is, it is crucial to understand its role within a NFA. It primarily serves two purposes:

1. A ε-transition enables a NFA to be more expressive, meaning it allows one to design compact automata while maintaining the same functionality. It aids in keeping the design simple, especially when modeling complex real-world problems where transitions may occur independently of the input.

2. Secondly, ε-transitions bring non-determinism into NFAs. An automaton can move to multiple next states for the current input or even without any input owing to these epsilon transitions, making the machine non-deterministic by nature.

What we then see is a path of logical evolution, where ε-transitions become extremely important when converting a regular expression directly to a NFA. This allows for more general composition to create non-deterministic machines that can capture wider classes of languages.

6.3. Decoding ε-Closures

A vital concept arising from the use of ε-transitions in NFAs is that of ε-closure. The ε-closure of a given state 'A' in a NFA is a set of states that can be reached from 'A' using only ε-transitions. It includes the state 'A' itself.

Calculated recursively, ε-closure paves the way for handling ε-transitions during the simulation of the NFA. By precalculating ε-closure sets, the computation overhead during the simulation can be significantly reduced, since we know beforehand the states an NFA can traverse using ε-transitions alone.

6.4. Practical Implementation Considerations

Understanding the theory behind ε-transitions and the implications they carry, it's time to delve into the practical side of this concept and address the considerations and challenges involved in implementing these transitions in code.

A common approach to handle ε-transitions is to navigate through the NFA states until an ε-transition is encountered and then adding all states achievable via ε-transitions to a set of possible next states.

This approach could be a potential performance bottleneck in large NFAs, due to the possible redundancies in calculating ε-closures in every step of transition.

A better alternative is to precalculate and store ε-closures of each state as part of NFA initialization and directly look up these sets during transition, thus reducing redundant computation.

6.5. Bridging Theory and Code

Once we've seen how important ε-transitions are for the design of NFAs, let's bridge the gap between theory and practice by writing a small piece of pseudocode which helps us calculate ε-closures for each state in NFA.

```
.Pre-calculating ε-Closures
[source,python]
```

function computeEpsilonClosure(nfa) is for each state in nfa do stack.push(state) while stack is not empty do current = stack.pop() for each neighboring state reachable via epsilon transition do if neighbor not in epsilonClosure(current) then epsilonClosure(current).add(neighbor) stack.push(neighbor) end if end for end while end for end function

This pseudocode reveals the simplicity behind the ε-closure: With a depth-first search approach, we can efficiently calculate the ε-closure for each state. Consequently, we can overcome the potentially intimidating task of handling ε-transitions in NFAs by remembering their expressive power and exploring practical and efficient coding methods.

A thorough understanding of ε-transitions and their

applications enables us to gain true proficiency in the domain of Non-deterministic Finite Automata. While NFAs may not be regularly used in everyday coding, they are integral to computational theory and, by extension, form the basis of regular expressions, text processing, and numerous applications in modern computing. As we navigate through the intricate world of computational theory, the ε-transition serves as a tool that intricately combines abstraction with functionality.

== Applications and Real-world Examples of NFA
Non-deterministic Finite Automata, or NFA, is intrinsically woven into a host of applications, some quite surprising. Throughout this section, we explore a plethora of NFA examples found in everyday life, its real-world manifestations, and how critical it is in software applications.

=== Pattern Matching and Regular Expressions

A prime application of NFA lies in pattern matching - more specifically, in the regular expressions used in computing. Regular expressions, also known as regex, are leveraged to search and manipulate text-based data, and NFA is integral to their internal functionality.

The goal of regex matching is to compare a string against a pattern, identifying all substrings that align with the prescribed pattern. It's a multidimensional problem: while the pattern size is generally small, the text to search might be considerably large. This calls for effective and efficient algorithms that can handle such voluminous data.

NFA comes into play as the critical technique used to

construct regex engines. It acts as a recognizer for the
targeted language and can be effectively utilized to
identify 'legal' strings that match a certain pattern.

Here's a basic illustration in code:

```python
import re
# defining a regular expression pattern
pattern = '^a...s$'
# defining a text to be searched
text = 'abyss'
# applying the pattern on text to find match
result = re.match(pattern, text)
if result:
  print("Search successful.")
else:
  print("Search unsuccessful.")
```

In above Python code snippet, we've employed the built-
in 're' module to work with regex. The 'match' function
attempts to match the defined pattern at the start of
the text. It searches for strings with length exactly
five, and the first character must be 'a', while the
last must be 's'. In this case, 'abyss' fits the bill.
Remember, underneath, an NFA is working hard to
recognize this language!

=== Automata in Lexical Analysis

NFA's also have prime importance in another computer
science field: lexical analysis, an essential part of
the compiler design process. Here, the source program is
divided into a series of tokens, which simplifies the
job of the parser in subsequent stages.

The lexical analyzer uses NFA (and its deterministic counterpart DFA) to recognize these tokens based on pre-set rules. As an example, tokens can be keywords, identifiers, operators, delimiters, and so on. With these token definitions, a lexical analyzer can identify a structure like an 'if' statement, addition operation, or a variable assignment in a source program.

Take a hypothetical token rule like "Variable names start with a letter, followed by zero or more letters or digits." An NFA can be constructed to recognize strings that meet this criteria, effectively identifying potential variable names in the codebase.

Its incarnation isn't limited to traditional programming languages and compilers. Specific tools like Lex - a lexer generator - use theory based on finite automata to identify and tag different parts of a string. It aids in creating routines in languages such as C or Ratfor to handle lexical patterns in text files.

=== Text Editors and Search Utilities

Text editors, beyond the apparent uses, can employ non-deterministic finite automata for implementing advanced features such as search and replace functionality. Many advanced text editors like Vim or Emacs use regular expressions, powered indirectly by NFA, for pattern search and manipulation.

Likewise, in the realm of command-line utilities, tools like 'grep' (a popular utility in Unix-based systems) utilize NFA to search for patterns in files or commands output. Essentially, `grep` functions as a practical, everyday application of regular expressions and, by proxy, non-deterministic finite automata. Be it software diagnostics or data filtering, the subtle application of theoretical computer science via grep cannot be overstated.

=== Network Intrusion Detection Systems

In the sphere of network security, NFA plays a crucial role as it helps create Intrusion Detection Systems (IDS). Generally, these systems inspect network traffic, trying to identify suspicious or malicious activity patterns.

NFA aids in building efficient pattern-matching algorithms for IDS. Patterns could involve signatures of known attacks or unusual data packets. An NFA-based approach enables the system to process multiple bits per cycle, enhancing the overall performance.

These real-world applications underline the profound relevance of NFA, reinforcing its robust foundations in the realm of theory while translating effectively into practical roles. The beauty of this core computational concept lies not only in its mathematical elegance but also in its utility and ubiquity in everyday applications. Whether it's simplifying complex tasks or empowering innovation, NFA's essence is truly an unsung hero in computational theory.

== From Theory to Code: Steps for Implementing NFA
Understanding the concept of Non-deterministic Finite Automata (NFA) is crucial for grasping foundational computer science theory. This chapter provides a step-by-step guide on how to translate the theoretical constructs of NFA into functional lines of code. We'll embark on a journey from theory right down to the

application in software development.

=== First Steps: Understanding the Basics of NFA

Before diving into the coding aspect, let's take a moment to understand the basics of NFA. By definition, an NFA is represented by five components: a set of states, the alphabet, the transition function, the start state, and the set of accept states.

The concept of non-determinism can be intimidating but isn't complex once understood. An NFA is considered to be non-deterministic because, unlike Deterministic Finite Automata (DFA), it can transition to multiple states for the same input, or even change states without any input at all!

The first step in implementing an NFA into code is to define these properties in your program.

Example:

```
class NFA:
    def __init__(self, states, alphabet,
transition_function, start_state, accept_states):
        self.states = states
        self.alphabet = alphabet
        self.transition_function = transition_function
        self.current_states = set([start_state])
        self.accept_states = accept_states
```

In this Python code, the class `NFA` is initialized by defining the five fundamental components of non-deterministic finite automata.

=== Building the Transition Function

The transition function in the NFA is a map from the
cross product of the set of states and the alphabet
(augmented with the empty string) to the power set of
the set of states.

Building the transition function depends heavily on the
specific task at hand. However, the foundation revolves
around ensuring that every input symbol reads the
current state and moves the machine to the next state(s)
in accordance to the function.

When reading an input symbol, the NFA may move to any
combination of the states in its set. Once the input is
completely processed, if the NFA has reached one of its
accepting states, the input string is accepted;
otherwise it is rejected.

Here is a simple implementation of a transition
function:

```
def transition_to(self, state, input):
    if (state, input) in self.transition_function:
        return self.transition_function[(state, input)]
    else:
        return set()
```

Remember, in Python, dictionaries or 'dict' objects can
behave like functions that are undefined for arguments
outside the domain.

=== Executing the NFA

The last step of implementing an NFA into code is designing a mechanism for the machine to make transitions and verify whether a given string is accepted or not.

The NFA 'reads' the string from left to right. It starts at the specified start_state and follows the path dictated by the transition function. At the end of the process (after reading the complete string), if the current state of the NFA is one of the accept states, the string is accepted. Otherwise, it's rejected.

A running_indices function can be defined, which is a helper function that recursively traverses possible paths of the NFA:

```
def running_indices(self, state, remainder):
    if remainder == "":
        return state in self.accept_states
    else:
        next_states = self.transition_to(state,
remainder[0])
        return any(self.running_indices(next_state,
remainder[1:])
                   for next_state in next_states)
```

The running_indices function operates as follows: when there is no remainder of the string left (i.e., all symbols have been read), it returns True if the current state is an accepted state and False if not.

=== Accepting or Rejecting String Inputs

Finally, we code the core acceptance function. This function reads the string and informs us if it's accepted or rejected.

```
def accept_string(self, str):
    return self.running_indices(self.start_state, str)
```

The function accept_string is a wrapper for
running_indices, to provide a clean API to the user who
shouldn't be bothered with providing the start state.

This chapter presented a broad overview of how to turn
theoretical NFA concepts into functional lines of code.
The step-by-step guidance should make the process
digestible and lead you to a successful implementation
of NFA. Remember, the NFA is a broad concept, and
different tasks might require different subtleties in
design. Stay flexible and experiment with the code to
fall in line with the problem at hand.

== Computer Programming Tools for Transcribing NFA
Understanding the abstract nature of Non-deterministic
Finite Automata (NFA) is just the first step in
mastering this critical concept in computer science
theory. The next crucial stride involves translating
this theory into usable code. To accomplish this piece
of the puzzle, you'll need appropriate programming tools
and a good understanding of how to leverage them to
transcribe NFA effectively. We're going to focus on that
in this section. Although several robust programming
tools can do the job, a few stand out as particularly
suited due to their simplicity, efficiency, and
extensive support communities.

=== Choosing a Programming Language

The first tool in your computer programming toolbox for transcribing NFA should be a powerful and flexible programming language. Although it's possible to implement NFA in any Turing-complete language, it's crucial to consider the language's features, readability, and tooling support for such complex computations.

Python is frequently the language of choice due to its simplicity and the extensive libraries available that allow the convenient construction of complex computer science structures. As a dynamically-typed language, Python provides great flexibility, making it perfect for implementing theoretical structures like NFAs.

Java is another excellent choice, especially for large and complex projects. The strongly typed nature of Java can bring some additional safety and predictability to your NFA transcriptions, while the object-oriented nature of the language aligns well with the state and transition structures of NFAs.

=== Implementing NFA Structures

The core of implementing a NFA into code is constructing an appropriate data structure to represent the automata itself. Usually, NFA's are represented as directed graphs where nodes represent states and edges signify transitions between states.

Before starting your implementation, ensure you have a clear understanding of the components that make up a NFA:

- A set of states, Q
- An alphabet set, ᚎ (Sigma)

- A transition function, δ (Delta)
- An initial state, q0
- A set of accept states, F

Each state has defined transitions based on the input
from the alphabet set. Reflect these relationships
accurately in your chosen data structure. Python
provides various options such as dictionaries, lists, or
even custom objects, while Java tend to favor more
structured options like HashMaps or custom state and
transition objects.

=== Algorithms for NFA Evaluation

Once your NFA structure is in place, the next step is to
write algorithms that evaluate given input strings
according to NFA rules. This functionality can be
partitioned into smaller functions: one that returns all
possible states after a single character is processed,
and one central algorithm that loops through all input
characters sequentially.

Your NFA evaluator should start from the initial state
and then follow transitions as dictated by the input
string. Remember, NFAs allow for multiple potential next
states for each input symbol, so your evaluator should
take this into account. Don't forget to handle the
possibility of epsilon or 'empty' transitions, where the
automata can transfer state without any input.

In Python, you might implement this with recursive
functions that return all potential states at each step.
In Java, a similar approach can be used, with recursive
methods that consider all potential state transitions.

=== Testing Your Implementation

Thorough testing is a crucial stage in every software project's life cycle. For NFAs, consistency and correctness checks should be performed to ensure your representation and evaluation functions as expected. Unit testing is a helpful strategy in this regard.

Python provides a built-in testing framework, `unittest`, while Java offers the widely-used `JUnit` framework. Both are robust solutions that allow the definition of test cases and automatic validation of results.

These programming tools facilitate the growth of your understanding through practical application, turning the abstract reality of NFAs into tangible code. Remember that practice is the perfect path to mastery and refer to community coding platforms if you encounter any stumbling blocks.

In the subsequent sections, we'll be dealing with more in-depth examples and see these tools in action. Up next, we explore the nitty-gritty of writing NFA algorithms and codes, with specific examples and detailed walkthroughs.

== Creating a Simple NFA: A Step-by-Step Walkthrough
Before we plunge into the details of creating a Non-deterministic Finite Automaton (NFA), it's essential to have a clear understanding of its different components. An NFA is characterized by five elements:

- A set of states (Q)
- An input alphabet (Σ)
- A transition function ($\delta : Q \times (\Sigma \cup \{\varepsilon\}) \rightarrow P(Q)$), wherein P(Q) refers to the power set of Q and ε

represents the 'empty string'
- An initial state (q0 ∈ Q)
- A set of final states (F ⊆ Q)

Here, we will create a simple NFA for the language that accepts strings ending with '101'.

=== Defining States and Input Alphabet

We will start with the creation of states and the variety of inputs they may accommodate. The idea here is to designate an object for each state and arrange them in such a way that their transition takes us to an acceptable endpoint (final state) for our input string.

```
[code]
states = ['q0', 'q1', 'q2', 'q3']

input_alphabet = ['0', '1']
[/code]
```

We defined four states ('q0', 'q1', 'q2', and 'q3'). 'q0' is the initial state, and 'q3' is the final. The input alphabet will be '0' and '1'.

=== Creating Transition Function

The transition function is a table that dictates the next state based on the current state and the input symbol. It accounts for every state-input pair, providing a guide for state navigation through our NFA given a string from our language.

Let's model the transition behavior by creating a dictionary in Python.

```
[code]
transitions = {
    'q0': {'0': ['q0'],          '1': ['q0', 'q1'],     'ε':
[]},
    'q1': {'0': ['q2'],          '1': [],               'ε':
[]},
    'q2': {'0': [],              '1': ['q3'],           'ε':
[]},
    'q3': {'0': [],              '1': [],               'ε':
[]}
}
[/code]
```

Each key refers to a state while the inner dictionary
defines possible transitions. For 'q0', an input of '0'
returns to 'q0', while '1' leads to itself or 'q1'. Our
final state, 'q3', doesn't transition anywhere else □
it's our endpoint.

=== Starting State and Final States

We need to determine the initial state and the final
states for our NFA. As per the previously fixed terms,
'q0' is our starting state, and 'q3' will serve as the
only final state.

```
[code]
initial_state = 'q0'
final_states = ['q3']
[/code]
```

=== Building NFA Simulation

Now, we have our set of states, input alphabet,
transition functions, initial state, and final states
ready. It's time to bind these elements and simulate our

NFA.

A detailed NFA simulator can involve recursion. For the first pass, we'll feed the NFA simulator with the initial state and start of the string. Each recursive call to the simulator then feeds in the following character in the string until we either land on the final state or exhaust the characters of our input string. If we land on a final state by the end of the string, we denote that the input string is accepted by our NFA. Otherwise, it's rejected.

Here's what this would look like in Python:

```
def NFA_simulator(current_state, remaining_string):
    # Base Case
    if len(remaining_string) == 0:
        return current_state in final_states

    # Recursive Case
    current_character = remaining_string[0]
    if current_state in transitions and
current_character in transitions[current_state]:
        next_states =
transitions[current_state][current_character]
        for next_state in next_states:
            if NFA_simulator(next_state,
remaining_string[1:]):
                return True
    return False
```

In this function, the base case evaluates whether our final state is in the list of 'final_states'. If it is, we return True (accept the string); if not, we return

False (reject the string). This triggers when we've consumed our input string.

The current character is read and compared against the transition dictionary. If there's a valid transition, it recursively calls 'NFA_simulator' for each, providing us different paths (the non-determinism in action!). The 'if' statement returns True once it finds an acceptance route, marking our string as accepted.

At a high level, creating a simple NFA is about demarcating states, enumerating the alphabet, formulating transition rules, and coding the acceptance criteria. The ability to transform these theoretical constructs into working code not only reinforces the understanding of the NFA model but also allows us to appreciate the practical applications and nuanced behaviors of NFAs.

== Exploring Complex Cases: Advanced Coding Techniques for NFA
As our exploration continues, we'll address more complex examples of Non-deterministic Finite Automata (NFA) and show how to translate them into practical code solutions.

=== Handling Nondeterminism in NFAs

Nondeterminism is a defining feature of NFAs. To handle this in a practical programming situation, we'll mostly use data structures known as 'sets'. In Python, you can represent sets using built-in language features. We'll also use the concept of a 'state'. Here's an abstract way of implementing these ideas:

```
[source,python]
```

```python
def nfa_to_dfa(states, alphabet, transition_function, start_state,
accept_states): dfa_states = [] dfa_transition_function = [] # other code
implementation
```

The purpose of this function is to convert a given NFA
into a Deterministic Finite Automaton (DFA) by following
the subsets method. We're using a list dfa_states to
keep track of all the DFA states, each of which is a set
of NFA states.

=== NFA with Epsilon Transitions

Epsilon transitions represent movements from one state
to another without consuming any input symbols. It's
such transitions that give NFAs their non-deterministic
character. In terms of coding, the task is to account
for these transitions. Here's a function that resolves
epsilon closures for a provided state:

```
[source,python]
```

```python
def epsilon_closure(state, transition_function): epsilon_set = {state}
for next_state in transition_function[state, ]: if next_state not in
epsilon_set:      epsilon_set      |=      epsilon_closure(next_state,
transition_function) return epsilon_set
```

In this function, we're forming a set of states that can
be achieved by only traversing epsilon transitions. We
exploit the property of sets in Python to ensure no
state is repeated in our set. We also use recursion to
ensure we capture all states, not just those immediately
accessible via epsilon transition, but also those beyond

the immediate reach.

=== Advanced Coding on Nondeterministic Finite Automata

Consider a scenario where you're analyzing a system's state, and it can be in one of many states at the same time. In coding terms, this is classic non-deterministic finite automata. In this case, recursion is incredibly useful. You may use a recursive function like this:

[source, python]

```python
def     move_to_next_states(current_state_set,     transition_char, transitions): next_state_set = set() for state in current_state_set: for next_state in transitions.get((state, transition_char), {}): next_state_set |= epsilon_closure(next_state, transitions) return next_state_set
```

This function is consuming one character of input and moving to all the possible next states, including the ones achievable via epsilon-transitions.

=== Converting NFA to DFA with Python

The final task in our coding manual represents the full conversion of our NFA to a DFA.

[source, python]

```python
def nfa_to_dfa(states, alphabet, transitions, start_state, accept_states): dfa_states = [epsilon_closure(start_state, transitions)] dfa_alphabet = alphabet - {''} dfa_transitions = {} dfa_start_state = dfa_states[0] dfa_accept_states = [state for state in dfa_states if state & accept_states]
```

```python
for from_state in dfa_states:
    for transition_char in dfa_alphabet:
        to_state = move_to_next_states(from_state,
transition_char, transitions)
        if to_state and to_state not in dfa_states:
            dfa_states.append(to_state)
            if to_state & accept_states:
                dfa_accept_states.append(to_state)
        if to_state:
            dfa_transitions[from_state, transition_char]
= to_state
```

```python
return dfa_states, dfa_alphabet, dfa_transitions,
dfa_start_state, dfa_accept_states
```

In the provided code, we're making use of the previously
presented helper functions. Note that we're building our
DFA dynamically, hence we're only adding new states to
dfa_states when we encounter an NFA state that we
haven't processed before.

In the end, you can clearly see the detailed process of
mapping an NFA's complex non-deterministic behavior into
a predictable deterministic model, shedding light on the
power and versatility of these concepts in real-world
programming instances.